☑ Review Content
☑ Action Planning
☑ Celebration
☑ Motivation

50

Creative Training Closers

Collected and Edited by
Bob Pike and Lynn Solem

Jossey-Bass
Pfeiffer
San Francisco

Creative Training Techniques
Press

Copyright © 1997 by Robert W. Pike and Lynn Solem

ISBN: 0-7879-3971-4

Library of Congress Cataloging-in-Publication Data
Pike, Robert W.
    50 creative training closers / collected by Bob Pike and
Lynn Solem.
        p.   cm.
    ISBN 0-7879-3971-4
    1. Employees—Training of. 2. Training. 3. Group games.
I. Solem, Lynn, 1934–   . II. Title. III. Title: Fifty creative
training closers.
    HF5549.5.T7P458   1997
    658.3'124—dc21   97-45301

Printed in the United States of America

Published by

350 Sansome Street, 5th Floor
San Francisco, California 94104-1342
(415) 433-1740; Fax (415) 433-0499
(800) 274-4434; Fax (800) 569-0443

7620 West 78th Street
Minneapolis, MN 55439
(800) 383-9210
(612) 829-1954; Fax (612) 829-0260

Visit our website at: www.pfeiffer.com

Visit our website at:
http://www.cttbobpike.com

Outside of the United States, Jossey-Bass/Pfeiffer products can be purchased from the following Simon & Schuster International Offices:

Jossey-Bass/Pfeiffer
3255 Wyandotte Street East
Windsor, Ontario N8Y 1E9
Canada
888-866-5559; Fax 800-605-2665

Prentice Hall Professional
Locked Bag 507
Frenchs Forest PO NSW 2086
Australia
61 2 9454 2200; Fax 61 2 9453 0089

Prentice Hall/Pfeiffer
P.O. Box 1636
Randburg 2125
South Africa
27 11 781 0780; Fax 27 11 781 0781

Prentice Hall
Campus 400
Maylands Avenue
Hemel Hempstead
Hertfordshire HP2 7EZ
United Kingdom
44(0) 1442 881891; Fax 44(0) 1442 882074

Simon & Schuster (Asia) Pte Ltd
317 Alexandra Road
#04–01 IKEA Building
Singapore 159965
Asia
65 476 4688; Fax 65 378 0370

Acquiring Editor: Matt Holt
Director of Development: Kathleen Dolan-Davies
Senior Production Editor: Dawn Kilgore
Editor: Rebecca Taff

Printing 10   9   8   7   6   5   4   3

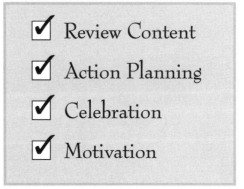

☑ Review Content
☑ Action Planning
☑ Celebration
☑ Motivation

This work is respectfully dedicated to participants who have attended the Creative Training Techniques courses and to the trainers: Dave Arch, Lori Backer, Michele Deck, Doug McCallum, Rich Meiss, Rich Ragan, and Tim Richardson.

And, to Bob Pike and Audrey Roholt—opportunity providers.

A special thank you to Vicki Solem for her tireless work in editing and entering.

And, to the staff of Creative Training Techniques, International: You do a million things right!

Lynn Solem

UNIVERSITY OF
GLOUCESTERSHIRE
at Cheltenham and Gloucester

**FRANCIS CLOSE HALL
LEARNING CENTRE**

Swindon Road Cheltenham
Gloucestershire GL50 4AZ
Telephone: 01242 714600

WEEK LOAN

Creative
Training
Closers

Contents

☑ Review Content

☑ Action Planning

☑ Celebration

☑ Motivation

Closers Matrix

☑ Review Content

☑ Action Planning

☑ Celebration

☑ Motivation

Closer	Review Content	Action Planning	Celebration	Motivation
A to Z Review	✓		✓	
Aspirin/Seltzer				✓
Barrier Balloons I	✓	✓	✓	
Barrier Balloons II	✓		✓	
Barrier Balloons III	✓		✓	
Breaking Barriers I	✓	✓		✓
Breaking Barriers II	✓	✓		✓
Candy Bar Paragraphs I	✓			
Candy Bar Paragraphs II	✓			
Colored Dots	✓	✓	✓	
Consulting Envelopes	✓			
Create a Quiz	✓			
Crossword Puzzle	✓			
Crossword Puzzle Race	✓			
CTT Quilt	✓		✓	✓
Envelopes on the Wall	✓			
Flying Missiles	✓	✓		
Foam Toys		✓		✓
Gallery Walk	✓	✓		
Geometric Close	✓			✓
Graduation	✓	✓	✓	
Junk Food Reminder	✓	✓	✓	✓
Keynote Review	✓			

Closer	Review Content	Action Planning	Celebration	Motivation
Laminated Question Cards	✓		✓	
Meiss Crumpled Paper	✓	✓		✓
Multiple Scribes	✓			
Name Tag Close	✓			
Object Lesson	✓			
Partial Mind Map	✓	✓	✓	✓
Pat on the Back			✓	✓
Pike's Pop-Ins	✓			
Pike's Power Tiles	✓	✓		
Pomp, Circumstance, & Clump	✓		✓	
Reflection Transparencies	✓			
Repetition	✓			
ROI	✓	✓	✓	✓
Role Plays	✓			
Sayings	✓			✓
Secret Support	✓	✓	✓	✓
See One, Do One, Teach One	✓			✓
Sixty-Second Commercial	✓		✓	
Skills/Knowledge Grid	✓	✓		✓
Stump the Participants	✓			
TABB Close	✓			✓
30/60/90-Mailback	✓			✓
3 . . . 2 . . . 1 . . .	✓	✓		✓
Top Ten Reasons to Use This Information	✓			✓
Transfer Vehicle	✓	✓	✓	✓
Transparency Teams Present . . .	✓			
Triad Support	✓	✓	✓	✓
Triad vs. Triad: Hangman	✓		✓	✓
Window Pane	✓	✓	✓	✓

Preface

☑ Review Content

☑ Action Planning

☑ Celebration

☑ Motivation

Any good presentation has an effective opening, a relevant middle, and a strong close. All too often when the presentation relates to training there is no close at all. The presenter simply runs out of time. "Oh, that's all we have time for. Thanks for coming. Oh, and be sure to complete the evaluation before you leave." Have you heard that before? Have you said it?

That short statement highlights much of what is wrong with the typical close in an average training program. At the same time it highlights the need for this book. What's wrong with the way many training programs close? Let us count the wrongs:

1. There is no close, they simply run out of time.

2. People are asked to give a hurried evaluation of the program as their last impression of the program.

3. Nothing happens to reinforce the key ideas of the program.

4. Participants have no opportunity to celebrate what they've learned.

Hopefully the techniques, tips, and actual closers we've provided in this volume will ensure that none of these things is true in a program you close. We've included the best techniques that we, as Creative Training Techniques trainers, have picked up over the past dozen years.

We've used all of them ourselves after learning many of them from others. Many of the closers were contributed by participants in one of our two-day Creative Training Techniques Seminars.

One thing you can be sure of—we've tried them all—and they work!

Whether your class is an hour long or several weeks long, you'll find closing ideas that will work for you. Whether you teach the most technical subject in the world or the most "touchy-feely" course imaginable you'll find a close that you can modify, adjust, adapt, and then adopt to your particular situation.

So, read, enjoy, and apply—and then give us your feedback.

Bob Pike

Introduction

☑ Review Content
☑ Action Planning
☑ Celebration
☑ Motivation

Closers

A major issue for trainers involves transfer of the learning or skill back to the work place. The landmark book, *Transfer of Training,* by Broad and Newstrom (1992) surprised the training world with research that showed that there was immediate transfer of only 40 percent of knowledge from training. Within six months, only 25 percent was retained; within one year of training, only 15 percent of the content was in use. The reasons are varied:

1. Technology changes. Perhaps the software has been replaced by an updated version.

2. Jobs change.

3. Management changes.

4. Products and systems change.

5. Employees return to face managers who say: "I don't care what they taught you! This is how we do it on the line."

One other reason that training does not transfer, the fact that a participant just does not remember what was taught, is addressed by this book.

In Bob Pike's book, *Creative Training Techniques Handbook* (1994), six components of memory are listed. Pike says that we remember those things that are: *outstanding*; that *link* to the known; that are *recorded* (written down by the person); that are *reviewed*; that use *primacy* (first or second position within the session); or that use *recency*.

You may have taken part in an activity during which the trainer reads off ten numbers and asks everyone to call out the first and last numbers from the list. Usually everyone can do this, but when asked to recall the seventh number, people have more difficulty. Often many different numbers are called out, many of them not even from the original list. The point is that people remember beginnings and ends. They forget middles. That is what "primacy" and "recency" mean.

As trainers we have long since accepted primacy as a concept. We make certain to open with something interesting and to state our major points up front in each session. Formal openings for a training session serve many purposes: they reduce tension, increase opportunities for networking, help to identify participant needs, and reinforce the concept of building a team. Openers are allocated a certain amount of time: for a one-hour session we might schedule five minutes. For a four-hour program, up to ten minutes. For an all-day program, up to twenty minutes. For a multi-day program, twenty to thirty minutes the first day, and up to ten minutes for each succeeding day.

Recency is addressed in this book by providing closers for trainers to use. Closers, too, have multiple purposes, not the least of which is to allow us to verify that what we have been trying to teach has been learned. Closers, however, are often neglected. One trainer we know, in response to the question, "How do you close a session?," replied: "I look at my watch. Say, 'Oh, oh, time's up! Good-bye.'" Unfortunately, this is true for many trainers. A participant in a recent class we held, when asked what he had learned, replied: "That closings are as important as openers! That's a new concept for me."

Closers are important not just because people remember endings. Pike (1992) recommends that every closer serve one of three purposes: to tie things together (revisit content); to form a basis for making action plans; or to celebrate the close of the training event. Additionally, closers often motivate participants to practice what they have learned when they return to the work place. Closers can be important to revisit the content, they can be exceptionally memorable, they can offer participants the opportunity to record their ideas, and they provide a link between what was taught and the work place. In fact, except for the fact that they cannot be first, closers serve every purpose and utilize every method to help participants remember them as openers do.

This book is filled with *practical* closers. Time frames and purposes are listed to enable you to "shop" for the close that best fits your needs.

Each closer is accompanied by the following illustration:

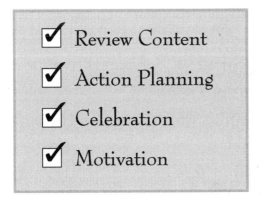

It has been designed to make it easy to see which closers are suitable for your needs.

Where known, we have included the source of the activity. We have also indicated the length of the training course that the closer is suitable for, the type of audience, size of group, and time and equipment needed.

In the next few pages we will address the following questions about closers:

    1. How does course evaluation fit into the close?

    2. What time frames apply to closers?

    3. How can games be used as closers?

Evaluation

We want participants to give thoughtful answers when evaluating our courses. If we wait until the course is entirely over to hand out an evaluation form, we may get less than a 100 percent response, and what we do get is probably not well thought through. To avoid these problems, some trainers have begun to give out evaluation forms before the close of training, even as early as the beginning. Some other reasons for handing out evaluation forms at the beginning are (1) to make participants aware of course content in general and (2) to point out key areas to be covered (a preview of content, a primacy technique, and an overview, all in one). Last but not least, handing out evaluation forms at the beginning of a course stimulates thought during the whole process.

Another good time to hand them out is early on the last day of a multi-day workshop. Or use extra time during a break on the last day for participants to complete the forms, making sure that participants understand that the course is not finished—that more important information will follow the break, or perhaps a celebration.

If you absolutely must wait until the end of the class to hand out an evaluation form, then a time just preceding the three components of closing (*tying everything together, making action plans, and celebrating*) can be dedicated to filling out the evaluation form. Avoid coming to complete closure and then introducing the evaluation form. In that case the evaluation process becomes anticlimactic and interferes with the principle of recency for the actual close.

Time Frames for Closers

If you have the same group of participants for three days, your openers may take twenty minutes the first day, fifteen minutes the second, and ten minutes the third. However, your closing times will *increase*. Utilizing the three components of closers: *tying things together, making action plans, and celebrating*, takes time.

Let's look at a possible closing scenario: To tie things together at the end of the first day, you might choose the "A to Z Review" (see page 7), which takes about eight minutes. From the information posted in the "A to Z Review" the participants could write down on 3" x 5" cards four things they will remember or implement within thirty days. Cards can be put in self-addressed envelopes; the trainer can collect the envelopes and mail them after thirty days. Now the class has revisited content and made action plans. The total time at this point would be about twelve minutes. An additional five minutes could be spent on celebration, such as drawing for prizes. The first day would end with a seventeen-minute close.

Time spent for a close must increase each day to take into account the growing amount of information that has been presented. On the second day, a round of "Jeopardy™" could be played. Thirty minutes could be allowed for a review of both days. On the third day, forty-five minutes might be allowed for "Trivial Pursuit™" or for a formal "Action-Plan Commitment."[1] If we think we just "don't have time" for lengthy closers, we only need to look at studies of what participants recall. Only about 20 percent of what has been told to participants is remembered (Kornikau & McElroy, 1975). Memory-enhancement activities simply *must* be included.

Games as Recall Tools[2]

In their outstanding manual, *G.A.M.E.S.: Getting Adults Motivated, Enthusiastic, and Satisfied,* Michele Deck and Jeanne Silva (1990) devote eighteen pages to games as valid teaching and learning tools. The methods games use include, among others, linking, chunking information, and repetition. Their companion games kit includes the

[1] The three activities mentioned here are from *G.A.M.E.S: Getting Adults Motivated, Enthusiastic and Satisfied* by Michele Deck and Jeanne Silva, published by Resources for Organizations, Minneapolis, Minnesota, copyright 1990.

[2] If there is resistance to using the word "games" in your training world, refer to these activities as recall exercises or as interactive learning activities. Whatever we call them, "games" are marvelous closers.

pieces needed to create learning activities based on six different well-known television game shows. Games are especially good for closing. This is particularly true in the case of technical information. Games encompass two of the three closing requisites: they tie things together and they add a feeling of celebration.

Many trainers use Jeopardy™-like games, but there are many, many other approaches. Variety is important for closers. Look at closers, whether games or not, as an opportunity to make sure that the transfer of learning has been enhanced and strengthened.

A to Z Review

- ☑ Review Content
- ☐ Action Planning
- ☑ Celebration
- ☐ Motivation

Objectives Fun, energizing revisit of content
Celebration

Class Length One-half day to one day

Audience Any group

Group Size Teams of five to seven participants; teams as small as three will work

Time 8 to 10 minutes

Equipment Newsprint Sheets
Masking Tape
Markers

Process It is essential to begin with the announcement that this is NOT a competition.

Each group chooses a scribe, who hangs the group's newsprint sheet on the wall. The scribe draws a vertical line down the middle of the sheet and prints the letters A to M down the left margin and N to Z at about midpoint on the sheet. (See example.) Teams gather around the flip chart and for each letter of the alphabet, they write a word or phrase from the course content.

If time allows, debrief by having scribes call out what their team has written for each letter. (*Note*: Be flexible! For instance: "X" might be used to mean something "x-tra.")

A	N
B	O
C	P
D	Q
E	R
F	S
G	T
H	U
I	V
J	W
K	X
L	Y
M	Z

Aspirin/Seltzer

☐ Review Content

☐ Action Planning

☐ Celebration

☑ Motivation

Source Participants in CTT courses

Objectives Motivation
To close with a visual impact

Class Length One-half day

Audience Any (although participants cannot be visually impaired)

Group Size Up to twelve participants

Time Approximately 3 to 5 minutes, timed by trainer prior to activity

Equipment Two identical glasses filled with water placed on a table that can be seen easily
An aspirin
A seltzer tablet

Process Trainer drops an aspirin in a glass of water, saying that no matter what training you have, if you don't do anything with it, it's like the aspirin in the water: Not much will happen.

Trainer drops seltzer tablet in other glass and says that if you take the skills and knowledge, the networking, and talent that has been part of the class and use them, it's like the seltzer tablet: Lots of things begin to "bubble up."

Barrier Balloons I

☑ Review Content

☑ Action Planning

☑ Celebration

☐ Motivation

Objectives Review course content
Make action plans
Celebration

Class Length One day

Audience Any

Group Size Any

Time 10 minutes

Equipment Slips of paper
Balloons (one per participant)

Process At the end of the course participants decide on one or more actions to take as a result of what they have learned. They share their ideas with their teammates.

Participants then identify their greatest challenges or barriers to using the new information, skills, or techniques.

Each barrier is also shared with the team, then written on a slip of paper. The papers are placed inside balloons, which are then blown up.

The balloons are tossed into the air and batted about by the participants. After approximately two minutes, each participant breaks the balloon closest to him or her to symbolize the breaking of the barriers.

Barrier Balloons II

☑ Review Content

☐ Action Planning

☑ Celebration

☐ Motivation

Objectives   Review content while having fun
Celebration

Class Length   One day

Audience   Any

Group Size   Minimum of four teams; teams of two are possible, but three to five participants per team is better

Time   12 minutes, including creating questions

Equipment   Slips of paper (five per team)
Balloons (five per team)
Modest prizes

Process   Divide content into as many sections as there are teams and assign one section to each team.

Each team reviews its assigned segment and writes five solid questions for which they know the answers. The questions are then put into balloons, one per balloon.

The balloons are blown up and tossed around the room for a few minutes.

Each team takes five of the balloons to its work area. In turn, each team breaks one balloon and tries to answer the question inside.

If a team is unable to answer a question, the team that wrote it answers it. Each team receives one point for each question answered correctly.

Give away modest prizes, such as candy bars, for the top teams, and gum for the other teams.

This is excellent after a one-day event, but will also work at the end of a one- to three-hour program or at the end of a key module.

Barrier Balloons III

☑ Review Content

☐ Action Planning

☑ Celebration

☐ Motivation

Objectives   Review content in fun way
Celebration

Class Length   One day

Audience   Any

Group Size   Minimum of four teams; teams of two are possible, but three to five participants per team is better

Time   8 to 10 minutes

Equipment   Slips of paper (five per team)
Balloons (five per team)

Process   Prior to the training, the trainer comes up with questions that will be answered during the course. Each question is written on a slip of paper and put inside a balloon. The trainer blows up the balloons.

During training, teams "win" balloons for such things as good ideas, coming back from break on time, etc. (*Note:* have a lot of balloons ready.)

At the end of the course, the balloons are broken and questions are answered by the teams. The trainer then gives points for correct answers and gives away modest prizes for each team, for example, candy bars for the top two teams and gum for the others.

Breaking Barriers I

☑ Review Content
☑ Action Planning
☐ Celebration
☑ Motivation

Objectives   Review course content
Make action plans
Motivate people

Class Length   One day

Audience   Any

Group Size   Preferably five teams; teams of two are possible, but three to five participants per team is better

Time   12 minutes

Equipment   Five sheets of flip-chart paper
Markers
Notebook pads and pencils for each participant

Process   Teams spend 3 to 5 minutes discussing barriers they feel they will encounter or have encountered that directly relate to the course (such as finding the time to attend, needing funds to purchase new equipment, or overcoming resistance from others), and write one barrier at the top of each sheet of newsprint.

The sheets are hung around the room. Each person takes a notebook pad and walks from one posted sheet to another, first reading what has been posted already so that duplicates can be removed. Then they write down the "barriers" that have been posted and try to come up with ideas on how to break them. This can be done during stretch breaks, between modules, or whenever the trainer wishes.

Breaking Barriers II

- ☑ Review Content
- ☑ Action Planning
- ☐ Celebration
- ☑ Motivation

Objectives   Review course content
Make action plans
Motivate participants

Class Length   One day

Audience   Any

Group Size   Preferably five teams; teams of two are possible, but three to five participants per team is better

Time   12 minutes

Equipment   Five sheets of flip-chart paper
Markers
Notebook pads and pencils for each participant

Process   After the lunch break of a one-day class or on the second morning of a two-day class, teams spend 3 to 5 minutes discussing barriers they feel they will encounter or have encountered on the job that directly relate to the content of the course (such as lack of time to implement new technology or low level of manager support) and write five of the barriers at the top of the newsprint sheets.

The sheets are hung around the room. Each person then takes a notebook pad and walks from one posted sheet to another, first reading what has been posted already so that duplicates can be removed. Then they write down the "barriers" that have been posted and try to come up with ideas on how to break them. This can be done during stretch breaks, between modules, or whenever the trainer wishes.

Candy Bar Paragraphs I

☑ Review Content
☐ Action Planning
☐ Celebration
☐ Motivation

Source   Creative Training Techniques participant

Objective   Review course content

Class Length   Up to one day

Audience   Any

Group Size   Teams of three participants each; any number of total teams

Time   8 to 10 minutes

Equipment   An assortment of miniature candy bars whose names lend themselves to training issues, e.g., PayDay®, Smarties®, 100,000 Grand®, Butterfinger® (for safety training), Twix® (for choice making), or 3Musketeers® (team building)

Process   Each member of a team is given the same candy bar. Working together they write a paragraph that ties that candy bar name to what they have learned. For safety training, for instance, if a team received PayDay® bars, their paragraph might begin as follows: In order to reach "Payday," it is necessary to be healthy . . . which means safety training is important.

Candy Bar Paragraphs II

☑ Review Content
☐ Action Planning
☐ Celebration
☐ Motivation

Source Creative Training Techniques participant

Objective Review course content

Class Length Up to one day

Audience Any

Group Size Teams of three participants each in any number of total teams

Time 8 to 10 minutes

Equipment An assortment of miniature candy bars whose names lend themselves to training issues, e.g., PayDay®, Smarties®, 100,000 Grand®, Butterfinger® (for safety training), Twix® (for choice making), or 3Musketeers® (team building).

Process Each member of a team receives a different candy bar and the team must create a paragraph describing key points in the training that weaves all names of the candy bars together.

An example for safety training might be: If you want to reach PayDay®, you need to turn all Butterfinger® into Smarties® with safety training. This is very good for one- to three-hour classes, especially in the afternoon (let them keep the candy) or at the close of any day or any module.

Colored Dots

☑ Review Content

☑ Action Planning

☑ Celebration

☐ Motivation

Source   Michele Deck

Objectives   Review all content
Action planning
Celebration

Class Length   Any

Audience   Any

Group Size   Any

Time   Ongoing during class, plus 15 to 20 minutes at the end

Equipment   Self-adhesive, removable colored dots, approximately ¼" in diameter (e.g., Avery™ 5795 ¼" Assorted)
The text or materials from the course

Process   Participants are given sheets of small multi-colored, removable adhesive dots early in the course. As the day progresses, they are to notice and place a dot next to good ideas, learning points, or things that would be beneficial to remember. Trainers can have "work breaks" so that participants can go over the latest sections of text and label the learning points. Each time they place dots in a section, they are reviewing content.

At the end of the class, everyone counts dots, and each participant lists the six things he or she will use first (which comprises an action plan) and the two most important learning points for him or her. These are shared with the team (or total group if the group is small enough). Small prizes can be given to the teams or individuals with the most dots.

Consulting Envelopes

☑ Review Content
☐ Action Planning
☐ Celebration
☐ Motivation

Objective   Fun, energizing review of content

Class Length   One half day or longer, up to one day

Audience   Any

Group Size   Any

Time   8 to 10 minutes

Equipment   One #10 envelope per participant
Several packs of 3" x 5" cards

Process   Each person puts his or her name on the front of an envelope, then writes a question or a request for information and/or resources underneath. During the course, the envelopes are passed from team to team. After each break, and after each module, the group spends 5 minutes coming up with as many solutions as possible to the questions on the envelopes that are on their tables.

To debrief at the end of the session, each participant takes the closest envelope and delivers it to the owner with the phrase: "Many happy answers." Each participant then shares one answer/resource from his or her envelope (in a large group, share with teammates; in a small group, share with the entire group).

Sample Envelope

Paul Presenter

I have a tight budget. What are some low-cost things I could take in to the classroom to liven up my training?

Create a Quiz

- ☑ Review Content
- ☐ Action Planning
- ☐ Celebration
- ☐ Motivation

Source   Bob Pike

Objective   Review content

Class Length   Any; excellent for one- to three-hour modules

Audience   Any

Group Size   Small

Time   Variable, depending on content

Equipment   Note pads and pencils for each participant

Process   At the beginning of the course, the participants are told that there will be a quiz at the end. After each module, participants are asked to develop two or three questions that would best sum up the learning points of that module. Questions are discussed (this gives a mini-review), then collected by the trainer. At the end of the course, all questions are turned into a quiz that the participants have created themselves.

As a variation and for additional review, after everyone has taken the quiz and it has been discussed, a quiz developed by another group can be discussed and/or taken. Participants can discuss the differences between their quiz and the other group's quiz, both positive and negative.

Crossword Puzzle

☑ Review Content

☐ Action Planning

☐ Celebration

☐ Motivation

Objective Review content

Class Length Any; excellent for one- to three-hour modules

Audience Any

Group Size Any

Time 10 to 12 minutes

Equipment One content-based crossword puzzle per person. (See following sample.) All may have the same puzzle, or a variety of puzzles may be used.

Process At the end of the course, give each participant his or her own crossword puzzle. Tell participants that for 5 to 8 minutes everyone will work alone. At the end of that time, each participant may consult with others to find any missing answers.

Variations Participants may work in pairs, triads, or teams to complete the puzzles.

After a specified period of time, the trainer can offer a printed listing, in alphabetical order, of all words used in the puzzle.

Sample Crossword Puzzle

Across Clues

2. Minimize this by holding programs off site.
7. Give frequent stretch breaks, but they must be _____.
8. A good brochure turns program outlines into program _____.
10. Clear questions can help you get answers that are _____.
11. A precise set of instructions for solving a problem.
13. Besides focusing on content, you want to focus on your _____.
15. Dressing a little better than is expected shows your audience _____.
16. Having an agreed-on master performer is one of two _____ for using observation for analysis.
17. When participants ask questions _____.

Down Clues

1. Promising _____ will help people give thorough, thoughtful, complete evaluations.
3. A good program announcement has a strong _____.
4. Visual aids provide this for a presentation.
5. One way of promoting networking is to use an _____.
6. One of the greatest needs of any human being.
9. Make sure the topics are useful and that each gets the right amount of _____.
11. Maximize the benefit of an outside speaker by making time _____ before and after.
12. Good evaluation questions stimulate participant _____.
14. Lack of eye contact can be caused by being _____.

Crossword Puzzle Race

☑ Review Content
☐ Action Planning
☐ Celebration
☐ Motivation

Objective   Review content

Class Length   One day minimum

Audience   Any

Group Size   Any; teams of three to five are ideal

Time   Varies, depending on content

Equipment   Modest prizes
Crossword puzzles (one per participant for small groups; one per team for large groups)

Process   Prior to the class, the trainer creates crossword puzzles (see sample from previous activity) that use the learning points from the text. At the end of the course, each participant (or team) receives a puzzle. The trainer has teams or individuals race to see who can fill in the puzzle first. (The same puzzle can be used for everyone if there is not enough information to create several puzzles, or a different puzzle can be used for each group.) Modest prizes are given to all.

CTT Quilt[3]

Source   Creative Training Techniques participant

Objectives   Review content
Celebration
Motivation

Class Length   Minimum of one day

Audience   Any

Group Size   Teams of six or more

Time   15 to 20 minutes

Equipment   Two sheets of flip-chart paper per team
Scissors
Masking tape
Clear tape
Markers of various colors for each team

Process   Each team hangs one blank sheet of flip-chart paper on the wall. They cut their second sheets into "quilt" pieces. Each team member receives his or her own piece and turns it into a visual representation of one

[3] *Note:* Use a title for this activity that fits the training, for example, "Conference Quilt," "Skills-Training Quilt," or "Enhance Customer Service Quilt."

key concept of the training, using the markers provided. (Members of the team should check with one another to avoid duplication.)

When the pieces are reassembled by taping them with clear tape to the sheet of paper on the wall, the quilt represents the team's combined visual efforts at recapturing learning. Participants should also explain to others what their quilt blocks represent.

Sample Quilt

Envelopes on the Wall

- ☑ Review Content
- ☐ Action Planning
- ☐ Celebration
- ☐ Motivation

Objective Fun, energizing review of content

Class Length Half day or longer, up to one day

Audience Any

Group Size Any

Time 8 to 10 minutes

Equipment One #10 envelope per participant
Masking tape
Several packs of 3" x 5" cards

Process Each person puts his or her name and a question or difficult situation related to the topic of training on the "flap" side of an envelope, but not on the flap itself. The envelopes are then hung on the wall with masking tape, questions showing, as shown in the illustration. During breaks, at lunch, or whenever the trainer feels it is appropriate, participants take some 3" x 5" cards and look at the questions on the envelopes. When they find a question they can answer, they put the answer on one of their 3" x 5" cards and put the card in the envelope. In this way, a participant might gather three or four possible solutions to a difficulty.

At the end of the class, participants retrieve their envelopes and read the cards. They choose one problem and its solution to share with their teammates.

Participants may also use their cards to network or to let their fellow group members know that they have extra information or resources that could help, by leaving their e-mail addresses and/or telephone numbers in the envelopes when appropriate.

Sample Envelope

TRICIA TRAINER

What do YOU do when you have 3 hours of content & 90 minutes of time?

Flying Missiles

☑ Review Content
☑ Action Planning
☐ Celebration
☐ Motivation

Source   Creative Training Techniques participant

Objectives   Review content quickly
Make action plans

Class Length   Up to one day

Audience   Any

Group Size   Any

Time   6 to 7 minutes (depending on how much review is needed)

Equipment   Paper and pencil for each participant

Process   Participants commit to take actions related to the content of the course and to do so by a certain date, usually two weeks to thirty days away. They write their action plans on sheets of paper, the dates by which they will take action, their names, and business telephone numbers.

They crumple their papers into balls and throw them into the air to celebrate their commitment to action. Each person catches (or finds) a crumpled paper that is not his or hers and tosses it up again, until three tosses have been made. At that point, each participant keeps the sheet he or she has and checks to make sure that it is not his or her own. Each participant commits to call the person whose action plan he or she received on the date shown on the paper. This can be a reminder to follow up on the action or it can be an offer of support.

Sample Missile

Name: _____

Number (including extension): _____

e-mail Address: _____

Date: _____

I will _____

Foam Toys

☐ Review Content
☑ Action Planning
☐ Celebration
☑ Motivation

Objective To commit to using the course material

Class Length Good for one- to three-hour sessions

Audience No more than twelve; participants must be able to see the trainer

Group Size Any

Time 3 to 4 minutes

Equipment A selection of foam toys encased in gelatin-like capsules[4]
A glass of cold water
A glass of hot water

Process The trainer experiments beforehand with the gelatin capsules, dropping one into cold water and one into hot water at the same time. His or her script for the lesson must be timed so that the word "transforming" comes at the same moment as the gelatin dissolves in the glass of hot water and a large foam toy emerges (very visibly) in the glass.

The basic message from the activity is that if you do not use the skills you have acquired during the session, your power to impact change in your organization will be like dropping one of the gelatin capsules into cold water. But if you do use the skills you learned in the session, your power to impact change can be transforming.

[4] The selection of toys encased in gelatin available in toy stores includes everything from robots to farm animals. They can be matched to the content of the course.

Gallery Walk

☑ Review Content
☑ Action Planning
☐ Celebration
☐ Motivation

Source   Lynn Solem

Objectives   Tie things together/Review content
Action planning

Class Length   Up to one day

Audience   Any

Group Size   Any

Time   10 to 12 minutes

Equipment   Wall charts that have been created throughout a minimum of one day of training
Several packs of 3" x 5" cards or Post-it™ notes
One self-addressed envelope per participant (optional)

Process   At the end of each module (if appropriate) or four times per day, teams can build wall charts that include the ideas/skills covered in the preceding module. At the end of the day, participants take 3" x 5" cards or Post-it™ notes and walk around the room; they carefully read each chart and commit to actions based on the charts.

If appropriate, a trainer might ask each participant to choose one action off each chart. The participants write the actions they are going to take on their 3" x 5" card(s), which are then collected to be mailed to them later.

Variation   An alternative could be to record the actions appropriately in a planning book or on a calendar.

Geometric Close

☑ Review Content

☐ Action Planning

☐ Celebration

☑ Motivation

Source   Creative Training Techniques participants

Objectives   Reflect on information given
Review content
Motivation

Class Length   Up to half a day (4 hours)

Audience   Any

Group Size   Individual activity for any number of participants

Time   8 to 10 minutes

Equipment   A large sheet of flip-chart paper
Markers

Process   Trainer draws the following on the flip chart:
- A Square
- A Triangle
- A Circle
- A "Z"

Each participant is asked to do the following:

1. Find something in the training that "squared" with what they already thought and share it with others. (SQUARE)

2. Find something in the training that made them view something from a new angle and share it. (TRIANGLE)

3. Find some new piece of information that completed or "closed the circle" for them and share it. (CIRCLE)

4. List an action or a new approach they will now take and share it. ("Z")

Larger groups can debrief in teams; for smaller groups, the participants can share with the entire group.

Sample Flip Chart

 *What squared (agreed) with something you already knew?*

 *What did you see from a new angle?*

 *What did you learn that was new, that completed a circle of knowledge?*

 *What new direction will you go in? What action will you take?*

Graduation

☑ Review Content
☑ Action Planning
☑ Celebration
☐ Motivation

Objectives   Add fun and full participation to review
Make action plans
Celebration

Class Length   Minimum of one day

Audience   Any who receive a certificate at the close of training

Group Size   More than five participants

Time   15 minutes, although time will vary depending on the number of participants

Equipment   One 3" x 5" card or a Post-it™ note per participant
One graduation certificate (already filled out) per participant

Process   First, each participant writes two ideas for changes or actions that he or she will take "back home" on the 3" x 5" card. Then, participants receive graduation certificates that are NOT their own. Participants then circulate around the room, carrying their cards with them. When they find the people whose graduation certificates they have, they say, "I can give you this certificate if you will give me your two ideas."

After people share their ideas, the certificate holders congratulate them, shake their hands, and announce that they have graduated.

Sample Certificate

Junk Food Reminder

- ☑ Review Content
- ☑ Action Planning
- ☑ Celebration
- ☑ Motivation

Objectives Fun, energizing revisit of content
Motivate participants
Make action plans
Celebration

Class Length Half day or longer, up to one day

Audience Any group that works together in the same location on a regular basis

Group Size Any

Time 8 to 10 minutes

Equipment One piece of paper per participant
Markers

Process At the close of the course, each person takes a piece of paper and writes down the following:

- Name
- Nickname
- Favorite junk food (something portable, for instance, a candy bar or chips)
- One thing pertaining to the course that they will accomplish during the next thirty days

The papers are then crumpled and tossed into the air. The participants pick up or catch one and toss it again, repeat this two or three times, pick up the one that is closest, and check to be sure that it is not their own. In thirty days, participants send the crumpled papers and the following memo in the self-addressed envelopes. (If participants work at the same location, they can send a piece of the favorite junk food as a reward.)

Sample Reminder

Name:	*Jamie Doe*
Nickname:	*Jammer*
Junk Food:	*Chips*
My Goal:	*To master the new software program*

Keynote Review

☑	Review Content
☐	Action Planning
☐	Celebration
☐	Motivation

Objective Fun, energizing revisit of content

Class Length Multiple days (at least two)

Audience Any

Group Size Any

Time 8 to 10 minutes at end of day and 5 minutes at start of next day

Equipment Newsprint sheets (one per module of the program)
Post-it™ notepads (a different color for each team)
Masking tape
Markers, one color per group

Process As each module is completed, the trainer labels a sheet of newsprint with the topic name at the top and posts it on the wall. At the close of the day, teams are formed for each module that has been posted. Using their notepads, the teams list ten review points for that module. Each group then shares its topic and learning points with the rest of the participants, taping their notes to the newsprint or writing the points with a marker.

The next day, using the same colors from the previous day, each team visits the other newsprint sheets and adds any points they think are pertinent, using either sheets from their notepads or a particular color marker to identify their ideas. Then a quick general discussion can be held of learnings from the previous day or participants can walk around to review on their own.

Laminated Question Cards

- ☑ Review Content
- ☐ Action Planning
- ☑ Celebration
- ☐ Motivation

Source Cypress Fairbanks School District

Objectives Review content
Celebration of knowledge
Wholesome competition

Class Length One day or longer

Audience Any

Group Size Any

Time Throughout the program; the celebration closer involves counting up card values from cards collected all day

Equipment Color-coded 3" x 5" laminated cards with point values and questions written on them. For example, cards that are green contain questions about material from the first module or about material that was covered between 9 a.m. and 10 a.m.; blue cards contain questions from the second module or about material covered between 10 a.m. and 11 a.m.; and so on. For a one-day class with twenty participants, between one hundred and two hundred cards would be needed. For a ninety-minute class with ten participants, approximately sixty cards would be needed.
A basket to hold the cards

Process   Prior to the training class, the trainer should write questions about the material to be covered in each module or during each hour on the cards, one question per card. A point value should be assigned, if appropriate.

A certain number (perhaps one out of every six cards) could be a trivia question that is not content related. The cards are laminated and are taken to the class.

The trainer decides the criteria for giving out the cards, for instance: the first volunteer; someone who has a good idea; or one card per table or team after each module. Whatever the criteria, the trainer will want to announce it and make the question basket available at the end of the first module or the first hour. The trainer places about one-fourth of the trivia cards and the questions for the first module or first hour in the basket. When a participant draws a card he or she reads the question out loud and receives the point value (either for the individual or the team) if he or she can answer it. Whoever answers a question correctly keeps the card.

If a question cannot be answered, the card is placed back into the basket, although the trainer may answer it first. As the day progresses, the trainer adds trivia cards and cards for each module or hour to the basket.

Each time a question is read aloud, whether or not it is answered, it is still a review of content. The group begins to pay great attention to the information as the day progresses.

At the end of the course, all unanswered cards can be distributed for one final round of answers. Rewards are given to all, with the highest perceived value to the team or individual with the most points.

Trainer Notes: Because everyone must have an equal chance to answer questions, determine your distribution system carefully. This activity can be amended so that it will work with one-on-one training also.

Sample Card

What 3 steps must
be completed <u>before</u>
the drive unit is
turned on?

Meiss Crumpled Paper

- ☑ Review Content
- ☑ Action Planning
- ☐ Celebration
- ☑ Motivation

Source   Rich Meiss

Objectives   Review content
Make action plans
Motivate participants

Class Length   Any

Audience   Any group that works together

Group Size   Any

Time   6 to 8 minutes

Equipment   One piece of paper and a pencil per participant

Process   Participants write on their sheets of paper one action they will take in the next thirty days, based on the training experience. They share their commitment verbally with other team members, then crumple the papers and put them into their pockets, purses, or briefcases, agreeing to carry them for thirty days.[5]

---

[5] It is amazing how often one cleans out one's pockets, purse, or briefcase over a thirty-day period, thinking, "What's this crumpled. . . . Oh, yes!"

Participants also can ask fellow participants to see their crumpled sheets of paper when they are back in the work place. If someone does not have his or her sheet, a token "penalty" can be charged.

Multiple Scribes

☑ Review Content

☐ Action Planning

☐ Celebration

☐ Motivation

Source Lynn Solem

Objective Comprehensive review of content

Class Length At least one day

Audience An audience that has experienced a day of idea generation

Group Size Enough participants so that four or more scribes can be writing while twelve or more participants are seated with the materials (*Note:* We have used this with up to 120 participants and fifteen scribes.)

Time 15 to 20 minutes

Equipment Markers for each scribe
A flip-chart sheet for each scribe
Masking tape

Process Hang the flip-chart sheets on the wall and ask for volunteers to fill out each sheet. Each volunteer writes his or her name at the top of the sheet and vertically numbers one through five as shown:

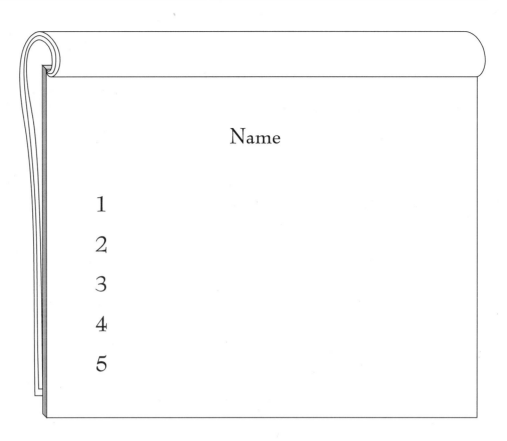

Participants who are seated are asked to go back to the beginning of their materials from the course and to page through, raising their hands when they come to a main point or a good idea. The trainer calls on people whose hands are raised and asks for their ideas, one at a time. Each idea is written by only one scribe, who takes down the idea while the trainer continues to the next person. The process continues, moving from scribe to scribe, until all ideas have been written on the sheets. By using this process, a group can surface more than seventy ideas in about 15 minutes, reviewing the content of the entire course.

Name Tag Close

- ☑ Review Content
- ☐ Action Planning
- ☐ Celebration
- ☐ Motivation

Source Lynn Solem

Objectives Complete review of content

Class Length From ninety minutes to one day; most effective when used in classes from one to three hours

Audience Any

Group Size Twelve or fewer

Time 12 to 20 minutes depending on the amount of content

Equipment Name tags with prepared questions written on them

Process At the beginning of the class, the trainer distributes one name tag per participant. Written on the name tag is a key question that will be covered during the course. Each participant is told to be especially watchful for the answer to the question he or she is wearing and to help others recognize the answers to questions they are wearing.

After these instructions are given, each person reads the question on his or her name tag aloud to the rest of the group. (This previews the course content.) At the end of the class, each participant stands, rereads his or her question, and states the answer. All participants help decide whether the answer is correct or not. If it is not, someone else may answer.

Object Lesson

☑ Review Content
☐ Action Planning
☐ Celebration
☐ Motivation

Source Creative Training Techniques participant

Objective Review course content

Class Length Best with classes of one to three hours

Audience Any

Group Size Either teams of five or six, in which case the information is shared at team level, or a group of no more than twelve participants, in which case the information is shared with the total group

Time 10 to 15 minutes

Equipment A variety of objects: aspirin tins, measuring cups, action figures, Koosh™ balls, paper clips, or any others of the trainer's choice

Process All the items are placed on a side table. At the end of the course, each participant is asked to think about the training just completed, then go to the table, select an object, and make a connection between it and the course content. They share this information either in teams of five or six or with a larger group of no more than twelve.

Partial Mind Map

- ☑ Review Content
- ☑ Action Planning
- ☑ Celebration
- ☑ Motivation

Objectives Review content
Make action plans
Celebration
Motivation

Class Length At least one day

Audience Any

Group Size Any

Time Ongoing; at end of a day, 15 to 20 minutes

Equipment Transparency of a partial mind map
Copies of a partial mind map for each participant (In a larger class, one per team)
A flip chart and markers

Process As prework, the trainer produces a partial mind map of the class, detailing the major learning points from the course.

The trainer has two options:

1. To fill in the major points and to give participants a number of blank lines to complete the map. (See sample at end of activity.)

2. To fill in the major points and to leave empty space so that participants can decide for themselves where to place lines and what to fill in. (See second sample.)

The partial mind map is given out at the end of the first module. The participants add the key points and ideas from the module that was just completed and do this after each ensuing module. This gives participants a visual representation of the course, with key terms and important learning points and their connections.

At the end of the class, participants make a group mind map on a flip-chart sheet, combining all of their ideas and eliminating duplications. (This gives the class another review and allows them to incorporate other participants' ideas into their own mind maps.)

Partial Mind Map

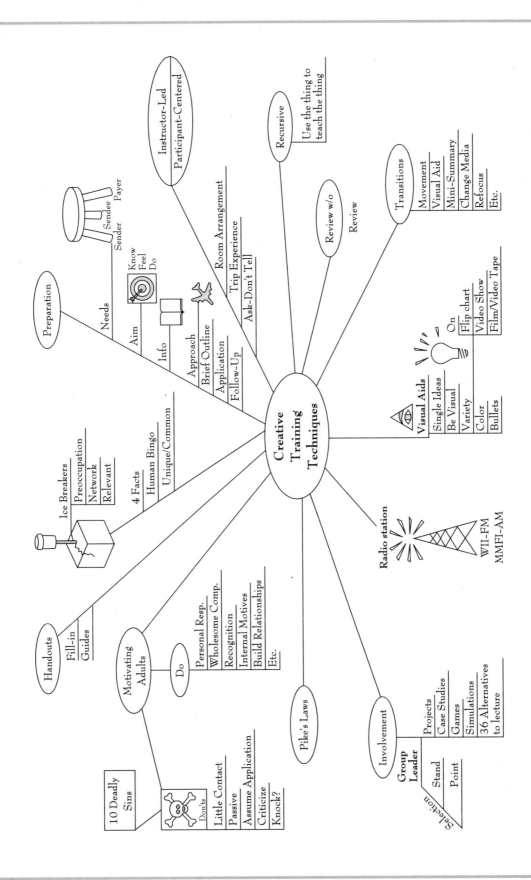

Creative Training Techniques

Preparation
Needs — Sendee, Sender, Payer
Aim — Know, Feel, Do
Info
Approach
Brief Outline
Application
Follow-Up

Instructor-Led / Participant-Centered
Room Arrangement
Trip Experience
Ask-Don't Tell

Recursive — Use the thing to teach the thing
Review w/o — Review

Transitions
Movement
Visual Aid
Mini-Summary
Change Media
Refocus
Etc.

Ice Breakers
Preoccupation
Network
Relevant
4 Facts
Human Bingo
Unique/Common

Handouts
Fill-in
Guides

Motivating Adults
Do
Personal Resp.
Wholesome Comp.
Recognition
Internal Motives
Build Relationships
Etc.

10 Deadly Sins
Don'ts
Little Contact
Passive
Assume Application
Criticize
Knock?

Pike's Laws

Visual Aids
Single Ideas
Be Visual
Variety
Color
Bullets
On
Flip chart
Video Show
Film/Video Tape

Radio station
WII-FM
MMFI-AM

Involvement
Group Leader
Stand
Point
Selection
Projects
Case Studies
Games
Simulations
36 Alternatives to lecture

Partial Mind Map

Instructor-Led
Participant-Centered

Recursive

Transitions

Preparation

Sendee
Sender   Payer

Know
Feel
Do

Review w/o
Review

Creative
Training
Techniques

Handouts

Motivating
Adults

Do

Pike's Laws

Involvement

Radio station

WII-FM
MMFI-AM

10 Deadly
Sins

Don'ts

Pat on the Back

☐ Review Content
☐ Action Planning
☑ Celebration
☑ Motivation

Objectives   Celebration
Motivate participants

Class Length   Minimum of one day (bonding must have occurred)

Audience   Any

Group Size   Groups as small as twelve and as large as 120

Time   20 minutes

Equipment   One ream of 8½" x 11" paper
Masking tape
Water-based markers (so there is no bleed-through)

Process   The trainer puts on each table a stack of white paper and a several rolls of masking tape (participants will be asked to tear pieces off as needed). The trainer asks for a volunteer and tapes one sheet of paper on that participant's back, then takes another sheet of white paper and tapes it over the first. The trainer then asks participants to help each other tape two sheets of white paper to one another's backs as demonstrated.

When everyone has finished, the trainer announces that there will be a celebration to honor one another. Using the water-based markers, all are to mill around the room, writing positive, supportive statements on the backs of as many people as possible in fifteen minutes.

Participants are asked to conserve space by writing small (but legibly), but they are also told that another sheet of paper may be added to a participant's back. After fifteen minutes, participants may read what has been written and share their feelings about it with one another, if desired.

Variation Teammates may remove the sheets, fold them, and put them in self-addressed envelopes to be mailed in sixty days. (Participants usually laugh and groan when they realize they will not see what others have written for sixty days.)

Pike's Pop Ins

- ☑ Review Content
- ☑ Action Planning
- ☐ Celebration
- ☐ Motivation

Source   Lynn Solem

Objectives   Review content
Make action plans

Class Length   From one to two hours

Audience   Any

Group Size   Teams with five to twelve members

Time   10 to 12 minutes

Equipment   Bowls filled with Pop-it™ beads for each team or group

Process   During the session, participants are invited to take out a bead for each new idea or an idea they would like to implement later. (They may want to identify the idea in their course materials as they go.) As they take each bead, they connect it to the previous bead(s), making a chain of knowledge or an action list. At the end of the course, participants are asked to put each bead back into the bowl one at a time, stating what idea that bead acknowledged. If one participant puts a bead into the bowl for a specific idea, and other participants have also taken a bead for that idea, all of them put their beads back into the bowl at the same time.

Pike's Power Tiles

☑ Review Content

☐ Action Planning

☐ Celebration

☐ Motivation

Source   Lynn Solem

Objective   Review content

Class Length   One to three hours

Audience   Any

Group Size   This can be an individual activity, done with learning partners, or done with teams of six or seven

Time   Time varies depending on the number of tiles each individual draws and whether the review is intended for one module of the training or for the entire session.

Equipment   One box of Pike's Power Tiles[6] per individual or team or one set of Scrabble™ tiles per individual or team, with some of the vowels removed

Process   The trainer determines the number of learning points to be reviewed.

---

[6] Pike's Power Tiles can be made by cutting out the letters on the sample sheet following this activity.

Each participant pulls that number of tiles out of the container and uses the tile as the beginning letter of the learning point (fact, process, information, or data) that is being reviewing. For example: The letter "P" can be used to remember the Preparation step or the letter "S" to remember Strategy or Safety.

A	A	A	A	B	B	B	B
B	B	C	C	C	C	C	C
D	D	D	D	D	D	E	E
E	E	E	E	E	E	E	E
E	E	F	F	F	F	G	G
G	G	H	H	H	H	I	I
I	I	I	I	J	J	L	L
L	L	M	M	M	M	M	M
M	M	N	N	N	N	N	N
N	N	O	O	O	O	P	P
P	P	R	R	R	R	R	R
R	R	S	S	S	S	S	S
S	S	T	T	T	T	T	T
T	T	U	U	U	U	V	V
V	V	W	W	W	W	Y	Y
Y	Y	S	S	S	S	S	S

Pomp, Circumstance, & Clump[7]

- [✔] Review Content
- [ ] Action Planning
- [✔] Celebration
- [ ] Motivation

Source Michele Deck

Objectives Recall material
Celebration

Class Length At least one day

Audience Any

Group Size A group of fifty or more

Time Depends on the size of the group

Equipment Cassette or disc player
Tape or disc of *Pomp and Circumstance*

Process At the end of the class, start the tape and ask each person, in turn, to stand to receive a certificate or to volunteer the best ideas they have learned. After each person receives a certificate or shares his or her ideas, the rest of the group claps one time—a clump—and the participant sits. Then it is the next person's turn.

[7] A "clump" is clapping that is lumped together into one clap (or clump).

Reflection Transparencies

> ☑ Review Content
> ☐ Action Planning
> ☐ Celebration
> ☐ Motivation

Source   Creative Training Techniques participant

Objective   Comprehensive review of material

Class Length   One hour to one day

Audience   Any group that has had a one- to four-hour training session using overhead transparencies as the main presentation tool

Group Size   Any

Time   As long as it takes to show each transparency for about ten seconds

Equipment   Overhead projector
Transparencies from the presentation
Cassette player
Soft music on cassettes[8]

Process   At the end of the class, the trainer plays some music and asks each participant to relax and look at a visual recap of the day. The trainer silently displays each overhead transparency in the same order as they were used earlier in the day for training. Each overhead is displayed for approximately ten to twelve seconds. The trainer remains silent.

[8] Use Baroque music or the Special Presentation Music listed in the Resources Section.

Note: People think faster (400 to 600 words per minute) than they speak (110 to 140 words per minute). If the trainer describes the transparency verbally, the participants' thought processes will be considerably slowed. If the trainer is silent, the participants will have the opportunity to recall all that was said previously about each transparency.

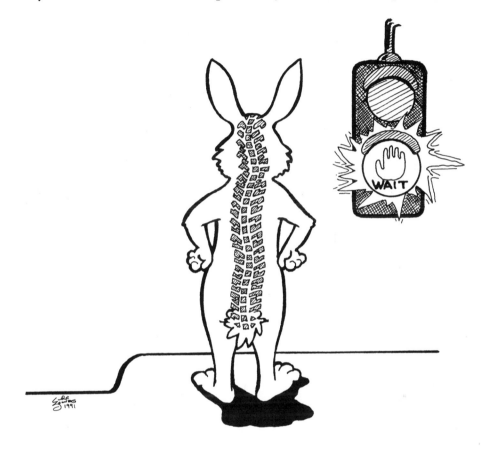

Learning has not

taken place until

behavior has

changed.

Taken from *Dreams.* Copyright © 1991, Resources for Organizations. Used with permission. All rights reserved.

Repetition

- ✓ Review Content
- ☐ Action Planning
- ☐ Celebration
- ☐ Motivation

Source Kodak trainer

Objective Review course material

Class Length Good for a one- to three-hour class

Audience Any

Group Size A team of five participants or multiple teams of five participants each

Time 7 minutes

Equipment None

Process Participants think of the main ideas they will take home from the event. They then number off from one through five. Beginning with number one, each participant says, "My name is April and one good idea I heard was . . ." (then tells what the idea is). Participant number two says, "April's good idea was . . . [and repeats it]. My name is Bill and one good idea I heard was . . . ." Participant number three would say: "April's good idea was . . . and Bill's good idea was . . .; my name is Carl, and one good idea I heard was . . . ." And so on until all participants have contributed.

ROI[9]

- ☑ Review Content
- ☑ Action Planning
- ☑ Celebration
- ☑ Motivation

Source   Michele Deck

Objectives   Review course content
Make action plans
Celebration
Motivate participants

Class Length   One day or can be adjusted for longer events

Audience   Any

Group Size   Minimum of eight participants, but works best in groups over twenty[10]

Time   12 to 15 minutes

Equipment   One self-addressed envelope per participant
At least two 3" x 5" cards per participant

Process   The trainer gives everyone at least two 3" x 5" cards and announces that they will be doing a four-part exercise. He or she gives directions for each part one at a time.

[9] ROI refers both to Return on Investment and to Retrieval of Information, as the return on investment in training is the participants' ability to retrieve the information when needed.
[10] This example is for four tables of five participants each for a one-day event.

Part 1: Each individual, silently working alone, reviews the entire content of the course and writes down four good ideas he or she has learned, two on each 3" x 5" card.

Part 2: Beginning with the group leader, each participant shares one idea from a card. If a participant did not write something down during Part 1, but thinks it is a good idea, he or she adds it to a card. This process is repeated around the table until each person has written down four more ideas, for a total of eight, four per card.

Part 3: Acknowledging the greater team (i.e., everyone in the room), all participants rise, find someone who was seated at a different table, and ask the person for one more idea. Then participants move to another person for one more idea. This continues until each person has added four more ideas, for a total of twelve per person, six per card.

Part 4: Participants return to their original groups, put their cards in self-addressed envelopes, and find partners who agree to mail the envelopes to them in sixty days.

Role Plays

- [✓] Review Content
- [ ] Action Planning
- [ ] Celebration
- [ ] Motivation

Objectives Skill practice
Review course material

Class Length Any

Audience Any for which role play would be effective

Group Size Any group divisible by three

Time Whatever is appropriate

Equipment Props appropriate to the role play
3" x 5" cards to identify the role (optional)
A bowl to draw roles (optional)
A script, if desired, or an outline of a situation or scenario may be given to the role players
Very clear instruction sheets must be used, containing time guidelines and a list of skills to be practiced

Process Group the participants into triads and assign them to be Observer, Role Player One, and Role Player Two.

Give the Observer a skills checklist (see sample on page 76) and instructions on what to watch for during the role plays.

Begin with Role Players One and Two conducting the role play while the Observer utilizes the checklist. Everyone may need instructions on giving and receiving feedback and also could be instructed to use the Sandwich Technique.[11]

The roles then rotate (see sample rotation on page 75), with each of the three participants playing each role once and acting as observer once. As roles are switched, the observer should debrief the other two, giving feedback and suggestions for improvement.

Notes:

1. People may be more comfortable using a name other than their own or simply being identified by job title or category, e.g., "newly hired marketing manager" or "angry customer." Appropriate and even outsize props can reduce tension during role plays.

2. If participants feel apprehensive about the process, the trainer may refer to the activity as "skill practice," rather than as a role play.

3. Roles can be drawn from a bowl if necessary so that participants do not feel "picked on" to play a negative role or to take the first turn.

[11] See Philip Hanson, Giving Feedback: An Interpersonal Skill, in the *1975 Annual Handbook for Group Facilitators,* © 1975 Jossey-Bass/Pfeiffer.

Sample Rotation of Roles

	Role One	Role Two	Observer
Round 1	Chris	Jan	Lee
Round 2	Lee	Chris	Jan
Round 3	Jan	Lee	Chris

Observer Sheet

During your role as Observer, use the following form to help you prepare your comments for the feedback session.

Instructions: Check the phrases that describe what you observe.

The role player(s)

_____	1. Helps to analyze problems.
_____	2. Helps to generate solutions.
_____	3. Acts as a clarifier to the role player(s).
_____	4. Acts as a summarizer.
_____	5. Contributes suggestions from experience and knowledge.
_____	6. Gives the role player(s) ready-made answers.
_____	7. Assumes the role player(s) has presented the problem accurately.
_____	8. Indicates attentiveness.
_____	9. Picks up on non-verbal cues.
_____	10. Talks more than the role player(s).
_____	11. Shows interest in the mentoree.
_____	12. Paraphrases.
_____	13. Confronts and/or challenges the role player(s).
_____	14. Collaborates with the role player(s) to define problem areas.

What seemed to be the most helpful thing the role player(s) said or did?

What behaviors seemed least helpful?

Other comments?

Sayings

☑ Review Content

☐ Action Planning

☐ Celebration

☑ Motivation

Source Lynn Solem

Objectives Review course in a fun way
Motivate participants

Class Length Any

Audience Any

Group Size Any

Time 12 minutes

Equipment Transparencies of motivational sayings
Copies of the transparencies on 8½" x 11" paper: in a small group, one saying per participant; for large groups, one per team (See samples following the activity.)[12]
An overhead projector

Process Prior to the class, throughout the training, and during breaks and lunches, display transparencies of motivational sayings with the overhead. At the end of the class, distribute the copies (for a small class,

---

[12]These are provided as samples only. Permission must be obtained for their use.

one per person; for a large class, one per team). Each participant (or team) then ties the motivational statement received to a learning point from the class. (For example, someone who is undergoing a company merger might use "We cannot change the wind, but we can adjust our sails" to discuss the situation and changes taking place.)

If new skills are being taught, transparencies such as "Progress always involves risk; you can't steal second base with your foot on first" can be used to acknowledge tension and risk, and to point out potential rewards from taking a chance. Once each person (or team) has an example, share with teammates or with the whole group, depending on time and size of group.

Leadership is action,

not position.

Donald H. McGannon

Progress always involves

risk; you can't steal second

base and keep your foot on first.

A turtle only moves
ahead by sticking
out its neck.

Your past is not your

potential. In any hour

you can choose to liberate

the future.

Marilyn Ferguson

We cannot

direct the wind...

But we can

adjust our sails.

Secret Support

☑ Review Content

☑ Action Planning

☑ Celebration

☑ Motivation

Objectives Review course material
Make action plans
Celebration
Motivate participants

Class Length Up to one day

Audience Works particularly well for a class that is learning behavioral change

Group Size Ten to twenty-five

Time 5 minutes

Equipment One 8 ½" x 11" sheet of paper and a pencil per participant

Process Trainer distributes paper to participants. Each participant writes down the following information:

1. Name
2. Daytime telephone number
3. Something he or she wants to accomplish
4. Something that would provide encouragement and support

Participants then crumple their papers and toss them into the air. They pick up a paper that is close and toss it again, then toss another. After three tosses, each participant picks up the nearest paper (making sure it is not his or her own).

At a set time (usually two weeks to thirty days from that day) the participants call the people whose papers they have and offer whatever support or encouragement was requested.

Example

Name: Lisa Chase

Daytime Telephone Number: 808–555–5555

What I would like to accomplish: Become less critical of my roommate

Encouragement I would like: Someone to listen to what I have tried so far and give me feedback.

See One, Do One, Teach One

☑ Review Content
☐ Action Planning
☐ Celebration
☑ Motivation

Source George Stanley, Hewlett Packard

Objectives Review course material
Ensure skill has been learned
Motivate participants

Class Length Any

Audience Any equipment-based or activity-based training group

Group Size Twelve or fewer

Time Dependent on skill to be practiced

Equipment Equipment involved in training

Process The name of this activity indicates the process: See one, do one, teach one. The old saying: "Tell them what you're going to tell them, tell them, then tell them what you told them" has been rethought for the modern learner and been changed to: "Tell them what you're going to tell them, tell them, then let them teach each other what they have learned."

This approach is effective for information giving and even more effective for building technical skills if a visual component is added: Participants *see* it done, do it, and then teach each other how it was done in pairs or in triads.

Sixty-Second Commercial

☑ Review Content
☐ Action Planning
☑ Celebration
☐ Motivation

Source Bob Pike's CTT Conference, Tampa, 1989

Objectives Review course material
Celebration of the training experience
Reinforce value of training

Class Length Works well with classes of one to three hours and when the content is "soft" skills

Audience Any

Group Size Teams of four to five

Time 6 to 8 minutes

Equipment Paper and pens or pencils

Process Each team is given 4 to 5 minutes to write a commercial promoting and selling the skills being trained. An example might be a commercial extolling the value of teamwork or a commercial on the value of using a certain communication process or the value of knowing company policies. Commercials might be written for the course workbook or for a video that was shown. (See sample commercial for CTT.)

Sample Commercial

Feeling those training blahs? Just can't get that old pizazz about a training program? Look for a Creative Training Techniques seminar! You'll network with other trainers, share ideas, learn new ways to motivate learners and how to deal with difficult participants. You can make a difference! Rejuvenate yourself now!

See you there!

Skills/Knowledge Grid

☑ Review Content
☑ Action Planning
☐ Celebration
☑ Motivation

Source Bob Pike

Objectives Review course material
Make action plans
Motivate participants
Check growth of skills and knowledge

Class Length Any

Audience Any

Group Size Any number of individuals working alone

Time 6 to 7 minutes per grid

Equipment Two performance grids per participant

Process *For new hires and for skills training*:

Prior to the class, the trainer develops a list of skills or learning points that participants can use to rate their own progress. At the beginning of the class, each participant receives a performance grid (see sample on page 92). Each participant ranks himself or herself, then puts the grid away. At the end of the class, the participants use another copy of the same grid to rank themselves again, then compare the two grids to see where they have gained in skills and knowledge.

For experienced personnel and training on soft skills:

The trainer can use a blank grid (see sample on page 93) and have the participants fill in the skills or qualities they think are needed. At the end of class, this serves not only as a review, but as a professional-development tool. After they have rated themselves for the second (and final) time, participants can list three areas for improvement and develop action plans to improve those areas of skill or knowledge.

Sample Grid for Customer Service	1	2	3	4	5	6	7	8	9	10
Appearance	·	·	·	·	·	·	·	·	·	·
Communication Skills	·	·	·	·	·	·	·	·	·	·
Courtesy	·	·	·	·	·	·	·	·	·	·
Empathy	·	·	·	·	·	·	·	·	·	·
Eye Contact	·	·	·	·	·	·	·	·	·	·
Friendly	·	·	·	·	·	·	·	·	·	·
Helpfulness	·	·	·	·	·	·	·	·	·	·
Knowledge of Job	·	·	·	·	·	·	·	·	·	·
Listening Skills	·	·	·	·	·	·	·	·	·	·
Reliable	·	·	·	·	·	·	·	·	·	·
Responsiveness	·	·	·	·	·	·	·	·	·	·
Positive Self-Image	·	·	·	·	·	·	·	·	·	·
Service Orientation	·	·	·	·	·	·	·	·	·	·
Smile	·	·	·	·	·	·	·	·	·	·
Willingness to Resolve Problems	·	·	·	·	·	·	·	·	·	·

Sample Blank Grid

Skills or Knowledge Needed	1	2	3	4	5	6	7	8	9	10
_____	·	·	·	·	·	·	·	·	·	·
_____	·	·	·	·	·	·	·	·	·	·
_____	·	·	·	·	·	·	·	·	·	·
_____	·	·	·	·	·	·	·	·	·	·
_____	·	·	·	·	·	·	·	·	·	·
_____	·	·	·	·	·	·	·	·	·	·
_____	·	·	·	·	·	·	·	·	·	·
_____	·	·	·	·	·	·	·	·	·	·
_____	·	·	·	·	·	·	·	·	·	·
_____	·	·	·	·	·	·	·	·	·	·
_____	·	·	·	·	·	·	·	·	·	·
_____	·	·	·	·	·	·	·	·	·	·
_____	·	·	·	·	·	·	·	·	·	·
_____	·	·	·	·	·	·	·	·	·	·
_____	·	·	·	·	·	·	·	·	·	·

3 Greatest _____   3 Greatest _____

1. _____   1. _____

2. _____   2. _____

3. _____   3. _____

Stump the Participants

- [✔] Review Content
- [ ] Action Planning
- [ ] Celebration
- [ ] Motivation

Source Lynn Solem

Objective Review course material

Class Length Any

Audience Any

Group Size Up to twenty participants

Time Varies depending on how technical the content is

Equipment Several packages of 3" x 5" cards each in two different colors

Process The trainer divides the group into two teams and gives 3" x 5" cards of one color to one team and a different color to a second team. He or she then divides the content of the course in half and assigns half to one team and half to the other. Participants review their assigned content, writing questions about the content and the answers on 3" x 5" cards.

After an appropriate time, the trainer gathers the cards and asks the first team to answer the questions from the second and vice versa. Points are given for each correctly answered question.

If a team is unable to answer a question, the trainer asks the team that wrote the question. If no one has an answer, the trainer gives the answer and puts the question at the bottom of the stack to be asked later.

Modest prizes are given to both teams.

Variation Particularly when training on a process or with a very small class, a variation of this, "Stump the Trainer" may be developed in which participants write questions for the trainer to answer.

TABB Close

✓	Review Content
☐	Action Planning
☐	Celebration
✓	Motivation

Source   Training for Impact

Objectives   Reflect on what has been learned
Promote ownership of learning
Motivate participants
Commitment at close of session

Class Length   Any

Audience   Any

Group Size   Any number of individuals working alone

Time   6 to 12 minutes

Equipment   One or two TABB sheets per participant

Process   Working individually, each participant lists the following (see sample TABB Form on page 98):

T: The most valuable *Thing(s)* being taken from the training

A: The *Action(s)* he or she will take because of the training

B: The *Barrier(s)* that may need to be overcome[13]

B: The *Benefit(s)* that will accrue from overcoming the barriers

[13]People will push through barriers such as lack of management support, lack of time, or bad habits for benefits they desire.

Participants then make commitments to overcome the barriers and to take action, sharing with others if desired.

Variation The TABB sheet copies could be mailed to participants thirty or sixty days later.

TABB Form

One of the most difficult things to do in any learning situation is to implement the ideas that were presented. Often this is because so many valid ideas are presented that it is nearly impossible to do something about each one—or even to remember what all of them were. This form can help you break the barriers of inertia and march toward achievement! The key is to focus on the most important idea presented and to decide to act on it.

T: What is the most important *thing* you learned from this session?

A: What *action* would you like to take on that idea?

B: What *barriers* stand in the way of your taking action?

B: What are the results, rewards, and *benefits* you would receive if you did take action?

Promise yourself that you will take action on what you have learned. Write all promises as positive statements. Check back on yourself at the end of ten days. Write the goal and a way to reward yourself on your calendar.

30/60/90-Day Mailback

☑ Review Content
☐ Action Planning
☐ Celebration
☑ Motivation

Source   Creative Training Techniques

Objectives   Review learning
Commit to action

Class Length   Any

Audience   Any

Group Size   Any number of participants working individually

Time   4 to 6 minutes

Equipment   Three 3" x 5" cards per participant
One self-addressed envelope per participant

Process   Each participant is asked to think of three ideas from the course that could be used as the basis for an action plan.

Participants print their ideas on the cards, along with first steps they would take to implement the plan, and put them into self-addressed envelopes to be mailed at thirty, sixty, or ninety days, depending on what is appropriate.

3...2...1...

☑ Review Content
☑ Action Planning
☐ Celebration
☑ Motivation

Source   Creative Training Techniques

Objectives   Review course
Make action plans
Motivate participants

Class Length   One and a half hours to one day

Audience   Any

Group Size   Any

Time   8 to 12 minutes

Equipment   Three 3" x 5" cards per person
One self-addressed envelope per participant

Process   Each participant takes one card and writes three things of value learned from the course, two things he or she will do the next day, and one thing the trainer could do to help on the card.

Participants copy this information onto each of their other cards and sign and date all three cards.

They take one of the cards with them; put one in an envelope to be mailed to them in a week; and give the other to the trainer, who contacts the participants to help as requested.

Sample Card

> ### 3 Things I Learned:
> How to write a topic sentence
> How to summarize at the end of a paragraph
> How to use attention-grabbing words
> ### I will do tomorrow:
> Write speech for next board meeting
> Make some note cards of good openers
> ### Would like from trainer:
> List of resources

Top Ten Reasons to Use This Information

☑ Review Content
☐ Action Planning
☐ Celebration
☑ Motivation

Source Creative Training Techniques participants

Objectives Summarize content
Plan results from learning

Class Length One day or more; works well for training as long as four or five days

Audience Works especially well for training on soft skills

Group Size Teams of three to seven members

Time 20 to 30 minutes

Equipment One flip chart with paper per team
Markers
Masking tape

Process Teams work together to come up with their "Top 10 Reasons" to use the information from the course. They write them on the flip-chart paper and post them for everyone to see.

Note: Ten is an arbitrary number. Five or twelve, or any number that works for the class, is fine.

Transfer Vehicle

☑ Review Content
☑ Action Planning
☑ Celebration
☑ Motivation

Source Tim Richardson

Objectives To have participants be creative as the session closes, while making decisions and commitments for the future

Class Length Half a day or longer

Audience Any

Group Size Teams of three to seven people

Time 12 to 18 minutes

Equipment Flip-chart paper for each team
Masking tape
Markers
One sample flip-chart sheet or overhead

Process Each team is given flip-chart paper, masking tape, and markers. They are instructed to draw a vehicle, anything from a horse and buggy to a star ship, to represent transfer of training.

Each sheet must show the team's vision (where they are going), the people involved, the baggage (what they are taking along), the motivation (fuel), and exhaust (what is being left behind). (See the example on page 104.)

Sample Flip Chart

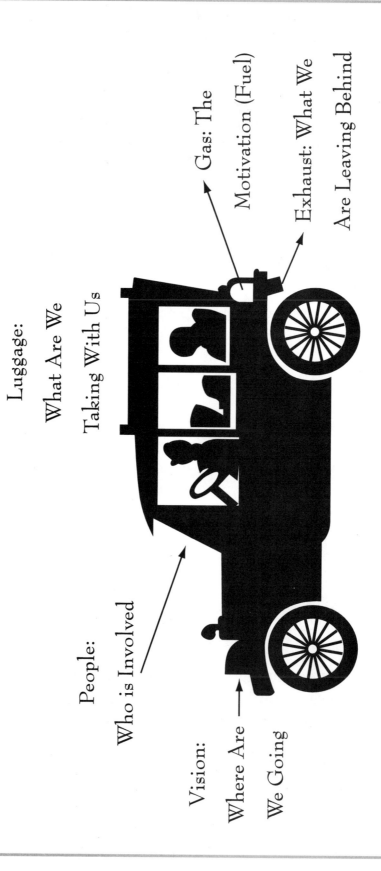

Luggage:
What Are We
Taking With Us

People:
Who is Involved

Vision:
Where Are
We Going

Gas: The
Motivation (Fuel)

Exhaust: What We
Are Leaving Behind

Transparency Teams Present . . .

- ☑ Review Content
- ☐ Action Planning
- ☐ Celebration
- ☐ Motivation

Objective Review course content

Class Length Three or more hours

Audience Any

Group Size Up to twenty, divided into teams of four or five

Time 15 to 20 minutes

Equipment Transparency pens and a box of transparency film
Overhead projector

Process Each team is assigned to review the content from the course and to outline the main points in memorable ways on transparencies for review by everyone.

For short classes, each team can be assigned to review the entire course. For courses that last more than half a day, the content can be divided among the teams.

Triad Support

☑ Review Content

☑ Action Planning

☑ Celebration

☑ Motivation

Source Bob Pike

Objectives Review content
Make action plans
Celebration
Motivate participants

Class Length Any

Audience Any group that works together at the same site

Group Size Any number divisible by three

Time 40 minutes

Equipment Handouts or a workbook from the class, as well as participants' notes

Process The trainer divides the group into three equal teams. Participants then number off in each group and make triads with the people with the same numbers in the other two groups.

For the last 30 minutes of the session, triads meet, each taking 10 minutes to discuss how they will use what they have learned and action plans they have made.

The triads agree to meet weekly for four weeks, at least half an hour per week, to discuss the challenges they have faced, to encourage each other, and to celebrate victories.

Triad vs. Triad: Hangman

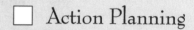

☑ Review Content
☐ Action Planning
☑ Celebration
☑ Motivation

Source Jenny Craig Trainers

Objectives Review content
Celebration
Friendly competition
Motivation

Class Length Up to one day

Audience Any

Group Size Six to twelve participants

Time As much time can be devoted to this as the trainer wishes

Equipment Flip chart with quadrille paper
Markers

Process Divide the class into two teams. Each team is to think of short phrases from the content that the other team will try to guess. The teams draw for which will begin, then draw blanks on the quadrille paper to represent letters in their phrase. (See page 109.)

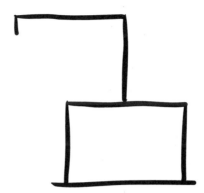

The second team guesses letters until either the phrase has been filled in or a stick figure is "hung," as shown below.

Note: When a letter is called out, every place it belongs in the phrase is filled in. Letters that are called out incorrectly must also be written visibly to avoid duplication.

Window Pane

☑ Review Content
☑ Action Planning
☑ Celebration
☑ Motivation

Objectives
Overview of course
Make action plans
Celebration
Motivate participants

Class Length One day

Audience Any

Group Size Any

Time 40 minutes

Equipment
Text and other learning materials
Flip-chart paper
Markers

Process The trainer divides course content into sections, one section per participant for a small class or one section per team for a large class. Each participant or team reviews the content and draws six or nine "window panes" to illustrate it on a flip-chart sheet. The window panes should utilize symbols or other graphics and illustrate the learning points as well as action plans. (See sample on page 111.) The group can debrief by having individuals or teams hang their sheets on the wall and explain them.

Sample Flip Chart

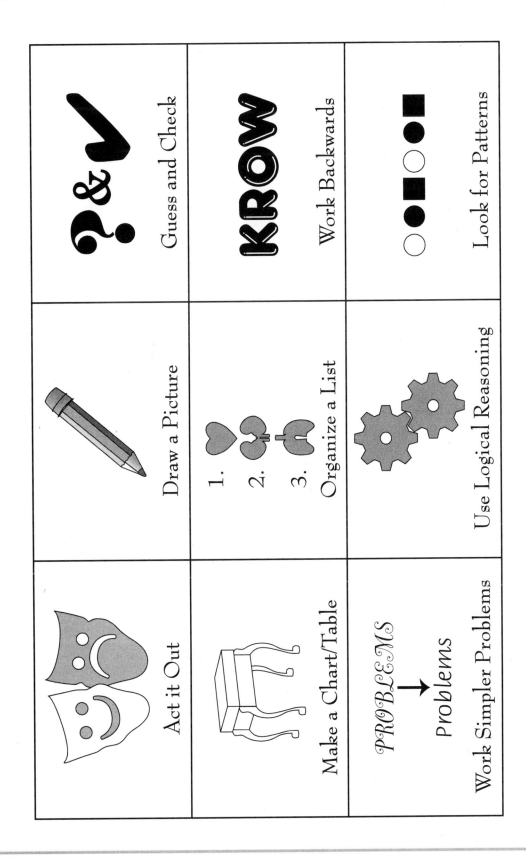

Act it Out	Draw a Picture	Guess and Check
Make a Chart/Table	Organize a List	Work Backwards
Work Simpler Problems	Use Logical Reasoning	Look for Patterns

Resources

☑ Review Content

☑ Action Planning

☑ Celebration

☑ Motivation

Broad, M.L., & Newstrom, J.W. (1992). *Transfer of training*. Reading, MA: Addison-Wesley.

Creative Training Techniques. (1992). *Creative Training Techniques playbook/workbook* (seminar material). Minneapolis: Author.

Deck, M., & Silva, J. (1990). *G.A.M.E.S.: Getting adults motivated, enthusiastic and satisfied* (manual & games kit). Minneapolis: Resources for Organizations.

Kaplan, D.E., & Kaplan, M.P. (1982) *Smiles*. Atlanta: Cheers Publishing Inc.

Kornikau, R., & McElroy, F. (1975). *Communication for the safety professional*. Chicago: National Safety Council.

Pike, R.W. (1994). *Creative training techniques handbook* (2nd ed.). Minneapolis: Lakewood Books.

Pike, R.W. (1991). *Dreams*. Minneapolis, MN: Resources for Organizations.

About the Authors

☑ Review Content

☑ Action Planning

☑ Celebration

☑ Motivation

Lynn Solem

Since December of 1986, Lynn Solem has delivered over 6,000 hours of Creative Training Techniques. She has delivered speciality aspects of Creative Training Techniques for Lakewood Publications *Best of America* and *Total Trainer Conferences* and for twelve different Education Service Centers and/or campuses in Texas. She is in the process of creating a professional video with one of the education service centers documenting the effectiveness of CTT on both educational staff developers (trainers) and classroom teachers.

As the former Executive Vice-President and CEO at Personal Dynamics Inc., she was responsible for developing and marketing materials used in seminars, training and workshop settings, as well as general operations. She has created and delivered seminars and workshops on such topics as sales skills, interpersonal communications, team building, leadership skills, communications styles, problem solving, and managing service as a corporate asset.

Lynn's training and/or consulting clients include a broad spectrum: General Dynamics, EDS, MCI Pacific and Midwest Divisions, IBM, Pennsylvania Power and Light, the National School Board Association, Southwestern Bell Telephone, and Consolidated Edison. In the manufacturing community, Lynn has done multiple trainings for Dupont, Kodak, and Hewlett Packard. In the service industries, AT&T, Continental, Delta, and Domino's Pizza. Public sector training includes

North Carolina Department of Social Services, Alabama Child Welfare, Ohio Early Child Care Providers, Federal Government Migrant Workers Head Start programs, the Coast Guard, the Air Force, U.S. Bureau of Patents, and the U.S. Postal Service.

Bob Pike, CSP

Bob Pike has developed and implemented training programs for business, industry, government, and the professions since 1969. As president of Creative Training Techniques International, Inc., and publisher of Creative Training Techniques Press, Bob leads sessions over 150 days per year covering topics of leadership, attitudes, motivation, communication, decision making, problem solving, personal and organizational effectiveness, conflict management, team building, and managerial productivity. More than 60,000 trainers have attended the Creative Training Techniques™ workshop. As a consultant, Bob has worked with such organizations as Pfizer, UpJohn, Caesar Boardwalk Regency, *Exhibitor Magazine*, Hallmark Cards, and IBM.

Over the years, Bob has contributed to magazines including *Training, The Personal Administrator,* and *The Self-Development Journal.* He is editor of the *Creative Training Techniques Newsletter* and is author of *The Creative Training Techniques Handbook* and *Improving Managerial Productivity.*

Bob Pike's
Creative Training Techniques™
Train-the-Trainer Conference

*The only conference dedicated exclusively
to the participant-centered approach to training*

- Learn about the revolutionary, participant-centered training approach—the breakthrough alternative to lecture-based training
- See the nation's leading training consultants model their very best participant-centered activities
- Experience the power of participant-centered techniques to dramatically increase retention
- Learn about innovative training transfer techniques adopted by leading Fortune 500 companies
- Discover powerful management strategies that clearly demonstrate the business results for your training programs

Just a few of the companies who have sent groups (not just individuals) to the Conference

American Express • AT&T • Caterpillar • First Bank
Southern Nuclear Operating Company • State Farm • United HealthCare • US West

Rave Reviews!

"I refer to my conference workbook all the time. I've shared the techniques with my trainers, and my own evaluations have improved. Our needs analysis now produces actionable input. My comfort level with our line managers has increased—at my first meeting with them where I used what I learned at the conference, they applauded. Now that's positive feedback!"
  Gretchen Gospodarek, Training Manager, **TCF Bank Wisconsin**

"For any trainer who wants to move beyond lecture-based training, I recommend Bob Pike's participant-centered seminars and in-house consultants."
  Ken Blanchard, Co-Author of *The One-Minute Manager*

"Bob Pike is creating a new standard in the industry by which all other programs will soon be measured."
  Elliott Masie, President, **The MASIE Center**

Visit our Web site: www.cttbobpike.com to learn more about the Conference,
Creative Training Techniques International, Inc. or the Participant-Centered Training approach.

1–800–383–9210
www.cttbobpike.com

Creative Training Techniques International, Inc. • 7620 W. 78th St., Mpls., MN 55439 • 612-829-1954 • Fax 612-829-0260

13 Questions to Ask *Before* You Bring Anyone In-House

An in-house program is an investment. You want to ensure high return. Here are 13 questions to ask before you ask anyone to train your trainers (or train anyone else!).

1. What kind of measurable results have other clients had from your training?
2. How much experience does this company have in training trainers?
3. Is this 100 percent of what the company does or just part of what it does?
4. How experienced are the trainers who will work with our people?
5. How experienced are your trainers in maximizing training transfer to the job?
6. Is the program tailored to my needs, or is it the same content as the public program?
7. Why is an in-house program to our advantage?
8. Is team-building a by-product of the seminar?
9. Is there immediate application of new skills during the training session?
10. What kinds of resource and reference materials do we get?
11. What type of pre-course preparation or post-course follow-up do you do?
12. How are our participants recognized for their achievements?
13. Will you teach my trainers how to get participant buy-in, even from the difficult participant?

Advantages of a Customized, In-House Program with Creative Training Techniques™ International, Inc.

Customized in-house programs provide your organization with training tailored to your specific needs. Our unique participant-centered teaching style is a revolutionary new training approach that is far more effective than traditional lecture-based training. This training approach has been adapted by a wide range of industries including healthcare, finance, communications, government, and non-profit agencies. Our clients include American Express, AT&T, Hewlett-Packard, 3M, U.S. Healthcare, and Tonka Corporation. We are eager to learn about your training needs and discuss how we can provide solutions. Please give us a call so we can help your company create a more vital and effective workforce.

Creative Training Techniques
International, Inc.

1–800–383–9210
www.cttbobpike.com

Creative Training Techniques International, Inc. • 7620 W. 78th St., Mpls., MN 55439 • 612-829-1954 • Fax 612-829-0260

More Great Resources from Jossey-Bass/Pfeiffer!

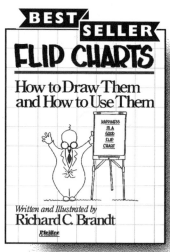

More Great Resources from Jossey-Bass/Pfeiffer!

Strengthen team bonds with friendly competition

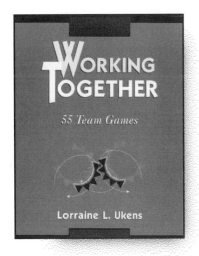

Working Together 55 Team Games
Lorraine L. Ukens

Take your team to a higher level of performance with a healthy dose of competition. These stimulating activities provide lessons in determination, teamwork, and planning—all critical elements in achieving high performance.

These simple games will help you:

- **Encourage** members to cooperate and use all members' abilities
- **Motivate** individuals to maximize their contribution
- **Demonstrate** the benefits of cooperative competition
- **Prepare** your team to meet future challenges
- **Emphasize** teamwork as a means to a solution as opposed to winning

Each game provides everything you need to conduct the activity including instructions, materials, time requirements, and reproducible worksheets or material templates. Each is categorized into one of these topics: change, communication, conflict resolution, data analysis, decision making, leadership, perception, problem solving, strategic planning, and time pressure.

Use these games to enhance cooperation, resourcefulness, decision making, efficiency, and initiative in your team today!

••
Working Together / **Code 0354X** / 224 pages / paperbound / **$39.95**

Start your training on the right track and keep it there!

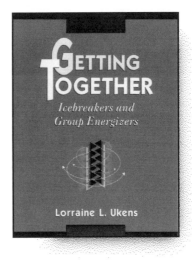

Getting Together Icebreakers and Group Energizers
Lorraine L. Ukens

These brief, interactive games and activities raise your participants' awareness and prepare them to learn something new. Designed to be fun and energizing, the activities help people overcome the initial anxiety common among new acquaintances or in group situations.

Use these games to:

- **Promote** interaction
- **Introduce** your topic
- **Ease** anxieties regarding sensitive or emotional issues
- **Form** partnerships or teams during the session
- **Help** people feel comfortable with the environment, the topic to be discussed, and one another
- **Gain** control of a group
- **Get** meetings started on a stimulating note

This collection is conveniently divided into two categories: 1) icebreakers, which encourage "mixing"; and 2) group challenges, which energize and build team cohesion.

Each game is presented in a concise and easy-to-follow format. You'll get details on objectives, material requirements, preparation, activity instructions, variations, discussion questions, group size, time requirements, and reproducible worksheets or material templates.

Use these icebreakers today to energize your group for the work ahead!
••
Getting Together / **Code 03558** / 224 pages / paperbound / **$39.95**